Plants
The Key to Life

Written by Kerrie Shanahan
Series Consultant: Linda Hoyt

WorldWise™
Content-based Learning

Contents

Introduction

What if there were no plants on Earth?

Think about these facts:

- Plants make their own food – humans and other animals cannot.

- We all depend on plants for the food and **energy** we need to stay alive.

- Plants produce most of the oxygen in the air that we breathe. Remember – trees are plants too!

REFORESTATION AREA

MACHINERY, DUMPING OR STORAGE OF ANY MATERIALS IS **PROHIBITED**

VIOLATORS ARE SUBJECT TO FINES AS IMPOSED BY THE MARYLAND FOREST CONSERVATION ACT OF 1991

How do plants do these amazing and important things? And, if plants are so important to us, are we looking after them?

Sadly, the answer is no. Many plants have disappeared from Earth, and many more are at risk.

Why are so many plants **endangered**? And what are we doing to save them?

Chapter 1

Why we need plants

Plants supply us with food and **energy**. They also supply us with oxygen that we breathe in from the air around us. We use plants to make medicines and many other products that we use every day.

Food and energy

Plants can do what no other living things can do – they can make their own food. How do they do this?

The sun is the source of all energy. Plants use the energy from the sun, as well as water and a gas from the air, to make their own food.

Find out more

The process of plants turning energy from the sun into food is called photosynthesis. Photosynthesis is a compound word (photo + synthesis). Find out what these two words mean. Think of other words that have *photo* or *synthesis* in them.

When an animal eats a plant, the energy stored in the plant is passed on to the animal. The animal uses some of this energy immediately, and some of it is stored in its body.

When animals eat other animals, they get the stored energy from the animal they have eaten.

This is called a **food chain**. We are part of a food chain.

Food chain

Energy from the sun

Grasses

Gazelle

Lion

In this grassland food chain, the grasses make their own energy using the sun's energy. Gazelles eat the grasses to get energy, and lions eat gazelles to get their energy.

7

Clean air

Not only do plants provide themselves and us with food, but they also provide us with oxygen. We need oxygen to breathe and live.

Plants take in a gas called carbon dioxide from the air and turn it into oxygen. They then put oxygen back into the air.

By taking in carbon dioxide, plants are cleaning the air that we breathe. Carbon dioxide can poison us.

The oxygen cycle

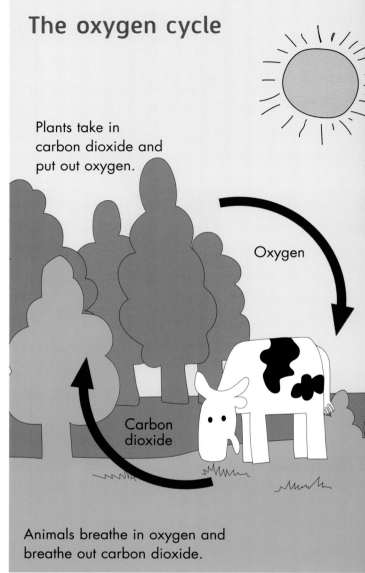

Plants take in carbon dioxide and put out oxygen.

Oxygen

Carbon dioxide

Animals breathe in oxygen and breathe out carbon dioxide.

Did you know?

Two fully grown trees produce enough oxygen to keep a family of four alive for a year.

Find out more

What are some other benefits from having trees growing near houses or buildings?

Cooling the world

Plants help to cool the world. They take in water through their roots. On hot days, the water is given off as water **vapour**. This cools the plant and the air around it.

Plants can protect us, too. They provide shade from the sun and protection from strong winds.

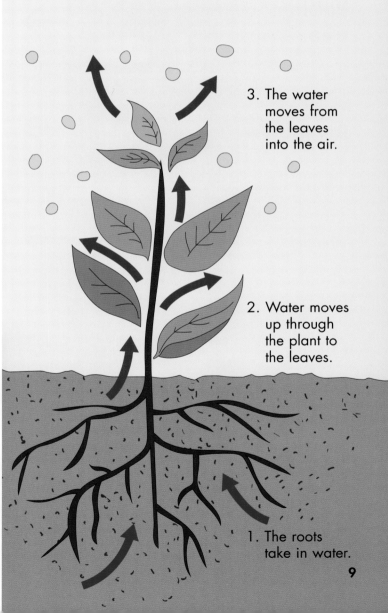

3. The water moves from the leaves into the air.

2. Water moves up through the plant to the leaves.

1. The roots take in water.

9

Products from plants

We use plants to make many of the things we use every day.

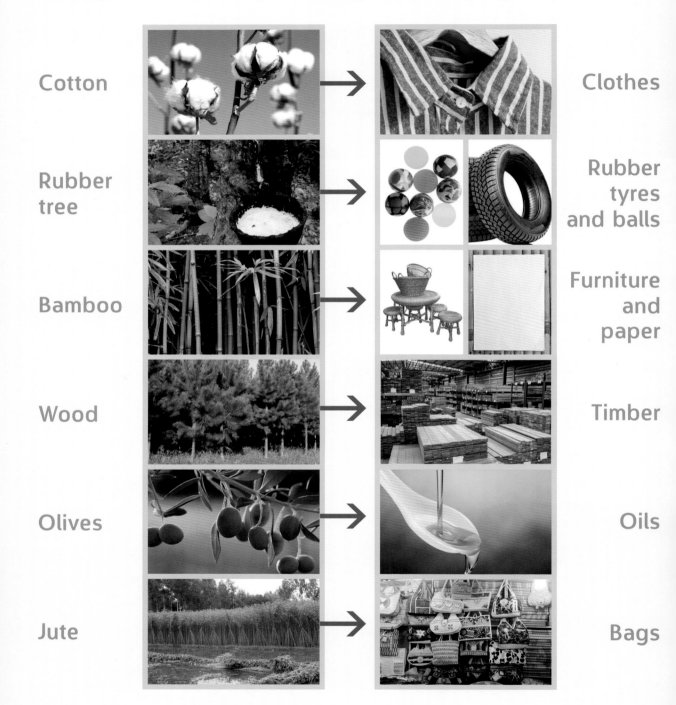

Cotton	→	Clothes
Rubber tree	→	Rubber tyres and balls
Bamboo	→	Furniture and paper
Wood	→	Timber
Olives	→	Oils
Jute	→	Bags

Plants provide medicines

For thousands of years, people have used certain plants to help them get better when they are sick. They discovered that different types of plants can relieve pain, heal cuts, or fix a stomachache.

	Garlic	Ginger	Eucalyptus leaves	Tea-tree leaves
Medicinal uses	Heart problems Cleans blood system	Stomach problems Infections	Body pains Fever and chills Sore throats	Sore throats Cuts and wounds Fungal infections
History	Ancient Egypt 3,200–343 BCE	Ancient Greece, Middle East, and China 2,500 years ago	Aboriginal and Torres Strait Islander peoples	Aboriginal and Torres Strait Islander peoples

Today, many of the medicines we use come from plants. Scientists have identified what is in many of these plants that works as a medicine. They use these plants to make medicines in a **laboratory**.

Chapter 2
Disappearing plants

We know that we need plants to survive. But we also know that many natural environments such as forests are being destroyed.

Why is this happening? Why are natural environments disappearing?

Clearing the land

The biggest reason for the loss of natural environments is people cutting down rainforests. People cut down forests, clear grasslands and drain **wetlands** to build houses, factories, roads and farms.

Animals such as the Borneo pygmy elephant (above left) and the puma (right) are **endangered** because the forests in which they live are being cut down.

Locusts eating the leaves of a crop

Natural disasters

Natural disasters such as bushfires, floods and cyclones can also damage plants and forests. Sometimes plants are so badly damaged that they cannot regrow, and large areas of vegetation are lost.

Pests and diseases can also destroy plants. This can happen quickly and in large numbers.

Pests such as insects can kill plants. For example, **locusts** can eat through vast amounts of plants. They do this quickly, and it can ruin natural environments.

Diseases can spread through plants. These diseases can kill off large areas of plants.

This banana plantation has been destroyed by a cyclone.

It can take hundreds of years for forests to recover from damage caused by bushfires.

13

Precious plants

Plants are important, but some are more valuable than others. And many of these valuable plants are being lost. The loss of these plants is important to animals, people and the environment.

Rainforests: Keeping the earth healthy

Rainforests provide us with clean air and fresh water.

Rainforest trees take in huge amounts of carbon dioxide from the air. This is important because too much carbon dioxide in the air makes the world hotter, and this damages the environment.

Rainforests are known as the lungs of the earth. They take in carbon dioxide and produce oxygen.

The Sumatran tiger is endangered because the forests where it lives are being cut down for timber or burned to make farms.

A rainforest in Sumatra is burned down to make way for farms.

Rainforest trees and other plants soak up water from the forest floor. This water is stored inside the plants and is slowly put back into the air as water **vapour** that helps to create rain clouds. The rain ends up in rivers and lakes. If this did not happen, droughts would occur more often, leading to food shortages and poverty.

Many rainforests are being cleared to make way for farms. And many trees are being cut down for their wood.

Without rainforests, the earth's climate will become much hotter and drier.

Find out more

- Rainforests take about 60 to 100 million years to grow and develop.
- Half of the world's land plant and animal species live in rainforests.
- Find a forest that is closest to you. What animals live there? Is this forest protected?

The roots of mangrove trees are underwater.

Mangrove forests: Protecting coastlines

Mangrove forests grow in coastal areas, where the land meets the sea. The roots of the mangrove trees hold the soil together. This stops it from being washed away by flooding, tides and waves.

These forests provide shelter for fish and other animals, and they protect people. They help to stop wind and the sea from damaging houses that are built on the coast.

But mangrove forests are disappearing. Many forests are being cleared to build shops and houses. Pollution is also killing the forests.

Without mangrove forests, the coastline will not be protected. And without mangrove forests, the animals and plants living there will not survive.

Rubbish in a mangrove forest

This mangrove forest is being replanted. People are planting young mangrove trees in the deep mud as part of the reforestation program.

Chapter 3
Protecting and planting

Many people know how important plants are and that there are laws to protect plants. These laws stop people from clearing natural environments such as rainforests or **wetlands**. Many people and organisations work to uphold these laws.

Some groups of people replant large areas of land. Others plant new plants in their homes, schools and communities.

Find out more

National parks have rules to protect the plants and animals living there. Find out about a national park near you. What rules does this park have?

A villager from northeastern Cambodia stands in a clearing where a tract of forest has been illegally cut down.

Fighting to save forests

Many people around the world are working hard to protect forests.

In Cambodia, a country in Asia, a man named Leng Ouch has been fighting to save forests for 20 years. He often works as a farmworker or truck driver so he can take photos and videos of illegal forest destruction. He then posts the images online so that the world knows what is happening.

Leng wants to stop local people from losing their homes and small farms. He works with them to protect the forests that still exist. His organisation is called Cambodia Human Rights Task Forces (CHRTF).

Replanting our trees

The first Australian Arbor Day was held in 1889.

Arbor Day is a day when people all around the world plant trees. In Australia, Arbor Day is observed on 20 June each year. On this day, groups of people work together to plant trees and shrubs. These volunteers help to replant forest areas, as well as planting new trees in parks, schools and other community areas in our towns and cities.

 Did you know?
The word *arbor* is from the Latin language and means tree.

NATIONAL

ARBOR DAY

Greening our cities

Many gardens are being planted in cities around the world. But some of these aren't your usual gardens. They are on the rooftops of city buildings.

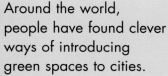

On top of the M Central apartment building in Sydney, Australia, there is a rooftop garden with **native** grasses, shrubs and trees. It is a relaxing outdoor area that is used by the people who live in the building, and their visitors.

Around the world, people have found clever ways of introducing green spaces to cities.

Find out more

Are there rooftop gardens in your closest city?

The garden reduces heat and cleans the air. Plants cool the environment by blocking sunlight and providing shade. They also put water **vapour** into the air. And they clean the air by taking in carbon dioxide.

The M Central rooftop garden was one of the first in Australia. Today, there are more and more rooftop gardens on city buildings throughout the country.

Conclusion

Without plants, we would not survive.

We use plants every day in countless ways. Knowing how important plants are, do you want to protect them? Why not join people from all around the world and begin replanting?

Let's replant the land.

Glossary

endangered an animal or plant species that is at risk of becoming extinct

energy fuel from food

food chain animals that depend on plants or other animals as a source of food

laboratory a room with special equipment for doing scientific experiments

locusts grasshoppers of a certain type

native belonging to a particular place

vapour a visible gas produced by heat

wetlands land areas that are covered with shallow water

Index